Creative Solutions

B. Vincent

Published by RWG Publishing, 2021.

CREATIVE SOLUTIONS

First edition. June 23, 2021.

Written by B. Vincent.

Also by B. Vincent

Affiliate Marketing
Affiliate Marketing
Affiliate Marketing

Standalone
Affiliate Recruiting
Business Layoffs & Firings
Business and Entrepreneur Guide
Business Remote Workforce
Career Transition
Project Management
Precision Targeting
Professional Development
Strategic Planning
Content Marketing
Imminent List Building
Getting Past GateKeepers
Banner Ads
Bookkeeping

Bridge Pages
Business Acquisition
Business Bogging
Marketing Automation
Better Meetings
Conversion Optimization
Creative Solutions

Table of Contents

Creative Solutions 1

Module 1 3

Module 2 9

Module 3 17

Creative Solutions

Hello and welcome to this course on finding creative design talent. In this course, we're going to cover how to find affordable creative design services. This course is divided into three modules. Module one covers the recently popular contest sites or bidding sites, module two covers traditional freelance services and module three shows us how to recruit permanent team members. By the time this course is over, you'll know how to effectively find creative talents for your business. So without further ado, let's dive into the first module. Okay guys, welcome to module one. In this module, our expert will cover contest sites or bidding sites. So get ready to take some notes and let's jump right in.

Module 1

So let's have a look at some of these contests or bidding sites. Let's start with 99designs.com. This is a cool website if you're looking for someone to design a logo or a graphics for your business. So on the website, you'll see the trending designs available such as the website builders, web page design, logo and brand identity pack. There are two ways to get a design. So you can work directly with a designer or start a contest and pay only once you pick the winner. So let's see how it works. Okay, so we have three steps here. The first one is preparing a simple brief or a design brief. So I went on to their FAQ to know how we can write a good design brief. So a good design brief includes the following. Number one, your brand and your business summary. So this can be two to three sentences stating about your brand and your business. Number two is the target audience. Here you want to say something like both men and women between the ages of 25 and 40 who are looking for outdoor adventures. Number three, we have the values to communicate with your design. So what feelings and messages do you want the visual design to communicate to your viewer? So in our example, we want to attract people who are looking for outdoor adventures. So we can design our graphics to showcase eco-friendliness, nature vibes and so on. Next, we have stylistic preferences. These are visual styles you want to achieve. Do you want artistic or bold or sophisticated and minimal? So this is your chance to let your designers know about your brand personality.

Next we have the colors. Color palette is part of your branding, so you need to prepare a color palette that reflects your brand and remember that these colors will represent you on any media that you use, so choose wisely. Next, we have example images. Here we can provide templates or inspiration images to our designer. Sometimes there's no better way to express our ideas than to show visual representation of what it looks like. So providing example images can really help our designer understand what we mean. Then we go back to our step. The next step is to connect. So as mentioned, we have two ways on how we can work with a designer. Number one is to hire a designer. You can hire a designer and collaborate with them directly, or you can start a contest. So for this example, let's say we want to start a contest. Let's click get started. So we need to select the category of which design we want to request or create. Let's choose logo and identity, and let's choose the logo and brand identity pack. Once you read through the details, you can now click start a contest. Next, we need to select a design for the designers to assess our style. So if you're looking for something modern, something minimalist, you can select from the choices here or you also have the option to skip this step. Here, you can adjust the slider depending on which requirement you really want. For example, if you want a more modern style, you can slide it a little bit here or all the way here to let the designer know the level of specific issue you want. If you want it to be more classic or more modern, you can slide it.

So let's say I want everything in the middle or let's say I want it to be sophisticated and economical, organic abstract, modern, I want it to be more modern. Once you're all set, just click continue, and then select the color palette. So here you'll see the brand description of each color. So I want to choose Aqua, maybe reds, then maybe for a neutral color—So you have the option to select three colors for your brand. So I want to select Aqua, reds and maybe neutral, then select continue. Once that is set, you are now going to provide your logo and brand or your business brand. So write your email, the language you want to write your brief in, your background information; What's the name of your logo? Do you have a slogan you want to incorporate in your logo? And describe the organization or the target audience of your brand, select your industry and then any other comments that you would like to communicate with your designers. And of course, if you have any images or sketches, documents that can be helpful to your designers. Once you've filled that in, click continue and you will now have to choose your design package. So all logo and brand identity pack packages come with a 100% money back guarantee. So we have the bronze. Here, you can expect 30 designs from the bidding. You have the silver, which contains 40 designs, a money back guarantee and larger design price. So more variety here. For the gold, you will have 50 designs, larger design price, and you will be working with mid and top level designers. And last one is the platform which has 40 premium designs, still has the money back guarantee, larger designer prize, top level designers only, you have prioritized support and then a dedicated manager.

So once you've chosen the design package that you want, let's say I wanted to choose bronze for now. You can now create a contest title for your contest. So you can check out examples here and then type your contest title here and then you can also select how you want to promote your contest. It can be a feature, can be a highlight or a blog entry, or you can have the power pack which contains all three of those promotions. And then you also have the contest options. For example, if you want it to be guaranteed or do you want it to be a private contest? So you can select that and the duration of your contest, do you want to run it for seven days, three days, two days or 24 hours, depending on what you need. After that, you will be directed to your account creation. Once you click continue, you'll be redirected to your account creation and the payment option.

Another bidding site that I want to talk about is hatchwise.com. So hatchwise is similar to 99 designs.com and let's see, once we click start, create a process, you'll select a logo or the type of contest that you want to host. For example, you want to have a logo design contest. They also have the same pricing packages, but I think more designs. So for example, for the bronze, you have 30 plus designs and you'll be working with five designers or five designers will be joining your contest or bidding. And then we have the silver, which has 70 plus designs, 15 designers, 150 price included. And this is the package price, contest price. We have the goal which has 130 designs, 20 designers. So depending on your design needs, you can choose which package best suits your contest. So let's see, start a logo contest. The design brief is similar to 99designs.com. You have your company information, your slogan, your company organization, and your target audience. You also have what you want to include, the ideas that you want to include in your design, where are you going to use this logo for; online, print, merchandise, billboards or shops, television or a screen? And of course they have a restriction on what you don't want to have in your designer. You also have the values. So if you want it to be more feminine, masculine, simple, complicated, and so on. You also have the option to select the logos that you want to not copy, but be inspired. You also have the colors to use in your design, same as 99design. You want to have a color palette and then other facts that you want to include as well as the type of file that you want to be included in your final output.

So just click continue, and then you will be redirected to the options. So what logo package would you like to have? You have here the number of designs and what you will be getting. So full ownership of one design industry files, 39 listing fee, $50 prize amount and you'll be working with as mention five designers with a minimum of 30 custom designs. And you have the second package, the third, the fourth, and the custom package. You also have the option for project upgrades and project visibility and privacy. Basically the same as 99designs.com. Once you click continue here, you'll be redirected to the payment page and that's about it.

Module 2

Welcome to module two. In this module, our expert will cover traditional freelance sites. So get ready to take some notes and let's jump right in.

All right, guys. So let's start by having a look at fiverr.com. So Fiverr is a marketplace for freelancers if you're looking for someone to do a one-time job for your project. There are two ways on how you can find freelancers here to work on a one-time project for you. The first step is by browsing through the seller profile according to the services available. You can use the search bar, or you can select from the categories here on top. Let's look at some of the profiles under graphics and design, then logo design. You'll have more filter options to choose from to find the right fit that you're looking for. Let's start with the logo options. You can select the logo style that you require, the file format that you want, the services that are included, and then just click apply. Next, we have the seller details where you can select the level of the seller. Let's quickly talk about Fiverr's level system. So the seller level system is based on three criteria, the customer satisfaction, on time delivery and the quality of service or output. So automatically when the seller signs up on Fiverr, they are labeled as a new seller. Then they become level one according to their requirements that they have achieved. For example, if they have completed at least 60 days as an active seller, they have completed at least10 individual orders and earn at least $400, maintain a 4.7 star rating, has 90% response rate, order completion and on-time delivery over the course of 60 days and if they don't receive any warnings over the course of 30 days, then they will be tagged as level one seller.

Next, we have the level two seller. Basically they are the ones who have completed at least 120 days as an active seller and have completed 50 individual orders and earn at least $2,000 the duration of that time and then here the benefits of being a level two seller. And then we also have the top rated seller. So this is an elite group of sellers who enjoy a growing number of exclusive benefits as they continue providing buyers with an overall excellent experience. So it's like an incentives program for sellers who will be offering quality services to the buyers. And then let's go back now to our profile. So here in the profile finder, we also have the seller details. So we've already talked about the seller level. We can also select sellers who can speak English or a specific language that we require, and we can also filter them according to location, and then just click apply. We can also filter them according to our budget, set a minimum and a maximum rate, then click apply. We can also filter them according to the delivery time that they can provide or assure us. So it can be an express 24 hours, up to three days, up to seven days or anytime, and then apply. On the right side, you have a toggle switch where you can select freelancers that are under the pro services or the premium service that Fiverr offers. You also have the option to select local sellers based on your location. And then you also have the option to select sellers that are online right now. So for example, let's select the profile card of this freelancer. So let's have a quick overview first. So here you'll see the sample or the preview of the samples of the freelancer, the name of the freelancer, the level, the name or the description of the service and the starting rate.

So let's click on the profile, once you're on the profile page of the freelancer, this is how it will look like. So first we have the overview. Let's have another example. Let's try this example. For example, this seller has three packages that's being offered. We have the basic package, the standard and the premium. So this is how the profile looks at the first glance. When you click the description tab, you will be redirected to the description of the gig. So it contains the specifications and the detailed information about it. You can also check the description of the seller, the bio, where she's from, average response time, members since when and the last delivery time. Next we have the package comparison. So these are the detailed information. So all the check marks means these are the inclusion or what are included in the packages and then we can just select according to the budget or our requirements. And we also have their recommendations. So here are the templates that they've worked on that maybe we can tell them we want something like this. You also have the FAQ where it includes the commonly asked questions, such as, for example, what are included in the revision, what's included in the kit, delivered logos, will it have a watermark and so on, and then accepting deliveries and other important details that are not covered in the description. We also have the reviews where it contains reviews or feedback from people that they have already worked with. So this is a good example of a seller profile that we can select. You also have the reading here and the order numbers in queue. And if we still have additional questions, we can contact the seller.

The other way we can select or the other way, the other option to find freelancers to work for us is by posting a request. So on this page, I have already logged into my account. And then on your profile, just click your profile icon and then choose post a request. You'll be redirected here and then you'll type the description of the service that you're looking for. You can attach files up to one gig and then select a category. For example, graphics and design, subcategory, logo and design and the style, it can be optional. And then once you place your order, when would you like your service delivered? We can say for example, three days, and then we can input our budget as $10, for example, and then click submit request. So this will now appear on the freelancers buyer requests and they will be the ones submitting proposals to you. So their responses should appear on your messages inbox.

So another site where we can find freelancers for one time job is upwork.com. It works similarly like Fiverr, but you can choose to work with individuals or an agency. So let's have an overview of the upwork.com platform. This is how it will look like. You'll see here the same setup like Fiverr, where you can choose categories of the one-time job that you are looking for. So let's say we want to look for design and we want to choose design. So once you click the category design, you will be redirected here where you can see all the suggested and recommended freelancers that you can choose from. Another way that we can look for a freelancer is by signing up or posting a job. So we do that by signing up. So let's sign up and create an employer account. For this example, let's say four, and then click continue. Continue with an email. Here, you need to type in your name, your last name, create your password, select the country or your location, and then click hire for a project. So it's important that you select hire for a project, that way this will be an employer account, and then create my account. Once you're logged in, your dashboard or your main page should look like this and if it doesn't look like this, just go to your main menu here and click jobs, my jobs, and you should be redirected here. The cool thing about this is they already have job templates available for you, which you can use when you post for a job for the first time. So for example, we are going to choose design and creative templates. Let's choose the basic job post templates here. For example, creation and editing of videos for social media platforms, select start here.

Automatically, since we selected the template, all the information will be populated. So step one is enter the name of your job post, this is the option that we have selected. It's now here. So it just changed the text inside of the curly bracket. For example, create or edit videos for company XYZ, job category or check if this is the right category for it and then click next. Next we have the job description. Same since we are using a template, you'll see here, the curly bracket, just replace that with the information that you want or that you need. For example, the deliverables needed, what do you need for this video project? You can also attach additional project files here up to 100 MB and then click next. Step three, what type of projects do you have? So let's say this is a one-time project. You also have the option to select for ongoing project or complex project. You can also add screening questions if you like or require a cover letter. So in this example, we won't be requiring. After that, we are going to select the skills. What skills and expertise are most important to you in the video production? Let's say I'm looking for someone who has expertise in an explainer video, maybe a screencast and intro or an outro. You can also have the option to select video editing software that they should be using. For example, there'll be premier pro or Adobe after effects. You can also select additional skills and expertise that are not included here in the first option. And if it's not included here, you can simply type here to search for the skills.

Next we have the level of experience your freelancers need to have. For example, are you looking for someone who are in the entry level, someone who's intermediate level or an expert level. So let's say entry level and then click next. You can also select an option for divisibility of this job. How many people do you need for the job? One freelancer, more than one freelancer. So let's select one freelancer and then anyone, and then you can also select talent preferences. Second to the last or actually the last one, we have the budget. How would you like to pay for your freelancer or agency? So the most popular option is pay by the hour. You also have the option to pay a fixed price, and set your estimated budget. Let's say five to $10, and you can also set your own hourly range or don't add any hourly range. How long do you expect this project to last? Let's say I want this or this project might last one to three months or less than a month since we are only looking for a video. Maybe this is a one-time video per month. Next, do you have a time requirement for this project? Do you want them to work more than 30 hours, less than, or you're not sure yet. Let's select I don't know yet and then next. Once done, review your post, the title, job category, description, the details of the project, expertise that you're looking for. You can simply click the pencil icon here to edit if you need to edit any information and then you can now select post a job and wait for the proposals to come in.

Module 3

All right, welcome to module three. In this module, our expert will show you how to recruit permanent team members. So get ready to take some notes and let's jump right in.

So for permanent team members for creative solutions, in our opinion, the absolute best place is onlinejobs.ph. There are two ways you can find the best workers on this platform. Number one, on the main page, you can check out profiles and resumes readily available to you. For example, let's select this one, certified public accountant. You'll see the information about them like their profile summary, their ID proof or identity verification score, if they are available to use time proof, their expected salary, educational background and experience, basic information about them, their skill summary and worker's skill set and their top skills and so on. Next, let's check out the main menu that you'll find when you check out onlinejobs.ph. So we have here the job seeker tab, how it works, pricing, real results, post a job, sign up and login. Let's check out job seekers. The job seeker tab contains the latest job post for job seekers. So they can type here the type of jobs that they're looking for and then click search. This is how it would look like on the job seeker site. So they have the option to filter the category. For example, office and admin, virtual assistant category, let's say human resource management and for employment type, they can select freelance, part-time, full-time and then click refine search results. So they should be able to find all office and admin virtual assistant job listings here.

Next, we have the how it works tab. We have three selection, employer FAQ, job seeker FAQ, and some blog posts on how to learn how to outsource in the Philippines. Let's select the employer FAQ. You will be greeted by John Jonas, the owner of onlinejobs.ph and then the steps on how you can successfully hire a virtual assistant in the Philippines. Step one, you can post a job or search resumes. Step two, find a perfect staff member by communicating via email, interviewing them, finding the perfect fit, offering them a job. And step three, you can hire and manage using time proof, easy pay for their payment and some other frequently asked questions. Next, let's check the job seeker FAQ. Here you'll find some of the frequently asked questions for job seekers. Then we have the blog post. How to grow your business with virtual assistant, basically the overall experience of employers and companies that use the online jobs.bh platform and then we have the pricing. So let's talk about the pricing a little bit. So we have three accounts. You have the free account, the pro account and the premium account. All three accounts use time proof, you can bookmark workers and easy pay. The only difference is the free account has some restrictions. You can check out the link here, why they do not have free trial anymore, but for the free account you can post three job posts, you have two days job post approval, you can view job applications, but you cannot communicate with the applicants or the workers.

For the pro account, you can read worker reviews to check out the best candidate, hire workers and contact 75 workers per month. For the premium account, this is I think for the bigger organization, you can hire workers, contact 500 workers a month, have unlimited background data checks, worker mentoring service, and video guide to outsourcing. Then we have the real results tab, which contains testimonials from employers and workers who have used onlinejobs.ph. And finally, it's time to post a job. So we first need to sign up and create our employer account. So let's select, I'm an employer, type in your full name, email address, password, agree to the terms of service and privacy policy, then click register. Since I already have a free account, let's log in. This is how your dashboard will look like or your account page looks like. You have your job posts sections, your pinned workers sections, hired workers section, the training academy for an additional fee. You can give your VA or virtual assistant some training that they need. You have access to easy pay, your guides for outsourcing and you can also refer a friend and the bottom part contains quick links to the platform. Let's now start posting for a job ad. Click add job post and fill out the job information. So for this example, we are looking for a virtual assistant. So virtual assistant, detail oriented and driven. Type of employment, since we're looking for a permanent team member, let's select full-time. For the job description, I've prepared a job summary, and duties and responsibility and for the wage or salary, let's say 500 per month. Required ID proof, let's say 65. Our email and then contact person.

Then we select job skills. For the primary skill, since we are looking for detail oriented and driven, let's select office and admin virtual assistant, and we want someone who can use Excel. For the secondary skill we want someone who has project management skill and who can do other project management. And then for the secondary skill, we want someone who can speak English or can communicate English. And then click submit for review. Since this is a free account, we need to wait two days, two working days for our post to be approved. And then once it's approved, this is how it would look to our job seekers. So they'll see the title, they can apply or bookmark it. They can see the type of work, the salary, ID proof needed and date it was posted. So all the information, as well as the skill summary. And on your account you can see your account status here, your job posting, your account settings, your time proof and you have the option to upgrade or to log out. Next, let's talk about your account settings. Once you click your account settings under the dropdown menu here, you'll see all the profile or your business information. You can type in your business name, your contact name, address, city, country, time zone, your zip code, telephone number, fax, and website, and then save the information. You also have the option to change your password and then save your login information. If you need any changes. Next, let's talk about time proof. For workers, they need to download the time proof app and for employers, they can start using it by inviting their team members. It's easy to install and it's always free.

So this is how the app looks like if you will be using it and how it works is step one, you need to provide an email address of your employees to use time proof. Number two, the workers download the time proof app and only workers download and install it because employers will be able to view it on the reporting data on their account page. So once the worker starts logging in and working the time proof app will be taking some screenshots of their screen and it will measure the productivity and the time spent on the job that they're working.

Don't miss out!

Visit the website below and you can sign up to receive emails whenever B. Vincent publishes a new book. There's no charge and no obligation.

https://books2read.com/r/B-A-QWUO-TZTPB

BOOKS 2 READ

Connecting independent readers to independent writers.

Also by B. Vincent

Affiliate Marketing
Affiliate Marketing
Affiliate Marketing

Standalone
Affiliate Recruiting
Business Layoffs & Firings
Business and Entrepreneur Guide
Business Remote Workforce
Career Transition
Project Management
Precision Targeting
Professional Development
Strategic Planning
Content Marketing
Imminent List Building
Getting Past GateKeepers
Banner Ads
Bookkeeping

Bridge Pages
Business Acquisition
Business Bogging
Marketing Automation
Better Meetings
Conversion Optimization
Creative Solutions

About the Publisher

Accepting manuscripts in the most categories. We love to help people get their words available to the world.

Revival Waves of Glory focus is to provide more options to be published. We do traditional paperbacks, hardcovers, audio books and ebooks all over the world. A traditional royalty-based publisher that offers self-publishing options, Revival Waves provides a very author friendly and transparent publishing process, with President Bill Vincent involved in the full process of your book. Send us your manuscript and we will contact you as soon as possible.

Contact: Bill Vincent at rwgpublishing@yahoo.com www.rwgpublishing.com

www.ingramcontent.com/pod-product-compliance
Lightning Source LLC
Chambersburg PA
CBHW030536210326
41597CB00014B/1168